S0-AJZ-567

CR

REVIEW COPY
NOT FOR RESALE

YOUR LAND
AND
MY LAND

We Visit

THE
DOMINICAN
REPUBLIC

John A.
Torres

SAN DIEGO PUBLIC LIBRARY
ISABEL SCHON COLLECTION

Mitchell Lane
PUBLISHERS
P.O. Box 196
Hockessin, Delaware 19707

3 1336 08568 9660

DOMINICAN
REPUBLIC

YOUR LAND
AND
MY LAND

Brazil
Chile
Colombia
Cuba
The Dominican Republic
Mexico
Panama
Peru
Puerto Rico
Venezuela

YOUR LAND
AND
MY LAND

We Visit

THE
DOMINICAN REPUBLIC

Copyright © 2011 by Mitchell Lane Publishers, Inc. All rights reserved. No part
of this book may be reproduced without written permission from the publisher.
Printed and bound in the United States of America.

Printing        1        2        3        4        5        6        7        8        9

Library of Congress Cataloging-in-Publication Data
Torres, John Albert.
  We visit the Dominican Republic / by John A. Torres.
      p. cm. — (Your land and my land)
  Includes bibliographical references and index.
  ISBN 978-1-58415-891-2 (library bound)
  1. Dominican Republic—Juvenile literature.  I. Title.
  F1934.2.T67 2010
  972.93—dc22
                                                        2010006561

PUBLISHER'S NOTE: This story is based on the author's extensive research,
which he believes to be accurate. Documentation of his research is on page 61.
    The Internet sites referenced herein were active as of the publication date.
Due to the fleeting nature of some web sites, we cannot guarantee they will all

# Contents

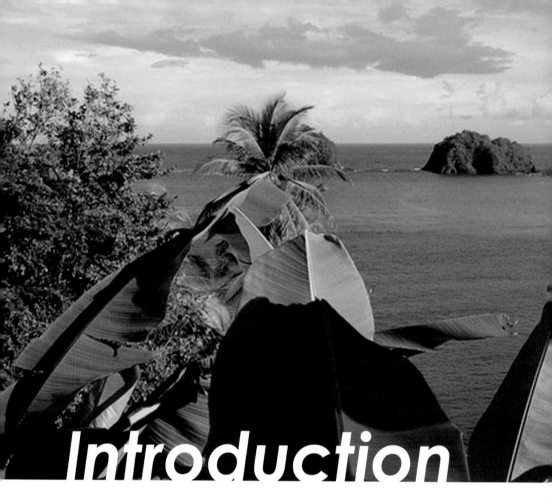

# *Introduction*

When people refer to the "Americas," they are usually referring to North America, South America, Central America, and even Latin America. While the first three—North, South, and Central—deal with geographic locations, Latin America is distinguished by its language. All the languages spoken in the countries that make up Latin America come from Latin. These include Spanish, Portuguese, and French. Nearly 600 million people live in Latin America, which ranges from the southernmost tip of Argentina in South America all the way to the border between Mexico and the United States.

There are about two dozen countries and territories that make up Latin America, including the largest country in South America—Brazil. Others include Haiti, the Dominican Republic, Mexico, Nicaragua, Chile, and Peru.

In this book we will be taking a closer look at the Dominican Republic, a country on the island of Hispaniola. This well-known part of Latin America became the home of explorer Christopher Columbus

during his later life. Not many people realize that after his discoveries in the Western Hemisphere, Columbus became the governor of the Dominican Republic, where he was considered both a hero and a tyrant.

**The regions and countries of Latin America include:**
*Caribbean*: Cuba, the Dominican Republic, and Puerto Rico
*North America*: Mexico
*Central America*: Belize, Costa Rica, El Salvador, Guatemala, Honduras, Nicaragua, Panama
*South America*: Argentina, Bolivia, Brazil, Chile, Colombia, Ecuador, Guyana, Paraguay, Peru, Suriname, Uruguay, Venezuela

Whether Christopher Columbus is buried in this lavish tomb in Seville, Spain, or in the Dominican Republic remains a point of contention between the two countries.

# Chapter 1

# Who Is Buried in Columbus's Tomb?

Welcome to the Dominican Republic!

Like many other Caribbean countries, this beautiful nation's history is tied closely to that of explorer Christopher Columbus and has a heavy Spanish influence. In fact, the country is located on the island of Hispaniola, which means "Little Spain." Its rich history includes many stories—and even mysteries—about Columbus.

How can there be a mystery about Christopher Columbus? Just wait and see. It's one that even the marvels of modern science can't quite solve.

Our journey starts at a beautiful plaza or park dedicated to the daring explorer. Just about everyone in the bustling capital city of Santo Domingo can tell you where to find Parque Colón (Columbus Square). Once there you will be greeted by dozens of pigeons looking for handouts and a huge bronze statue of Columbus himself.

Now take a look at the tall lighthouse nearby. Named simply Columbus Lighthouse, the structure is said to contain the remains of the famous explorer. The country of Spain, which colonized much of the Caribbean, including the island of Hispaniola, claims his bones are buried in a cathedral in Seville, Spain. Dominicans claim the bones are in their country. The debate is so fierce that the Dominican people allowed scientists to extract DNA samples for testing in 2003 to answer the question once and for all. The result? Even that is not clear. The DNA could be from Columbus, or it could be from someone in his family. Some scientists believe the bones were moved so many times that there could be some in the Dominican Republic and some in Spain.

What we do know is that Columbus, sailing with a small fleet of three ships from Spain, discovered Hispaniola just before Christmas in 1492. Actually, his crew did not have much choice about stopping there and exploring. One of his ships, the *Santa Maria*, ran aground just off the coast of the beautiful island. The bottom of the ship scraped against the ocean floor until it became stuck. If the water had been deeper, Columbus may not have stopped there and claimed the island.

Hispaniola has become home to two separate countries that speak two different languages. One country, the Dominican Republic, takes up the bulk of the island, and people speak Spanish there. The western third of Hispaniola is Haiti, where the people speak Creole, a language influenced by African dialects and French.

Directly to the east of the Dominican Republic is Puerto Rico, which is a commonwealth territory of the United States. To the west of Haiti is the island of Jamaica. To the northwest is Cuba. And many miles to the south is the northernmost tip of South America.

Like many of the Caribbean nations, the island was inhabited by Arawak and Taíno Indians before Columbus arrived. The area was ruled by the Spaniards for hundreds of years before finally winning independence, only to be conquered again and then subjected to very harsh rulers.

**FYI FACT:**

The Dominican Republic is the second largest Caribbean nation. Cuba is the largest.

The people in the Dominican Republic are very proud of their culture, as proven by their insistence that Columbus is buried there. The culture boasts influences from Europe and Africa as well as from its native peoples. They have developed rich and sometimes spicy foods, and great dance music such as the merengue style, with its infectious rhythms and catchy tunes. They

# THE DOMINICAN REPUBLIC FACTS AT A GLANCE

**Palm Chat**

**Full name:** The Dominican Republic
**Language:** Spanish
**Population:** 10.1 million (2009 estimate)
**Land area:** 18,656 square miles (48,442 sq km)
**Capital:** Santo Domingo
**Government:** Democratic republic
**Ethnic makeup:** Multiracial (73%), white (16%), black (11%)
**Religion:** Catholic (95%), Protestant, Spiritist, and other (5%)
**Climate:** Tropical
**Average temperatures:** August 90°F (32°C); January 60°F (16°C)
**Average rainfall:** 55 inches (140 cm)
**Highest point:** Pico Duarte (Duarte Peak)—10,128 feet (3,087 m)
**Longest river:** Yaque del Norte—184 miles (296 km)

**Flag:**

The flag was adopted in 1844. The blue and red are adopted from Haiti, which at one time controlled the Dominican Republic, and represent the struggle against Haitian rule. The blue stands for liberty and the red for the blood of heroes. The white cross is a symbol of freedom, peace, and salvation.

**National motto:** *Dios, Patria, Libertad* (God, Fatherland, Liberty)
**National flower:** The caoba—the flower of the mahogany tree
**National bird:** The palm chat. These brown songbirds can be found almost anywhere on the island of Hispaniola but love to congregate around palm trees.
**National tree:** The mahogony tree

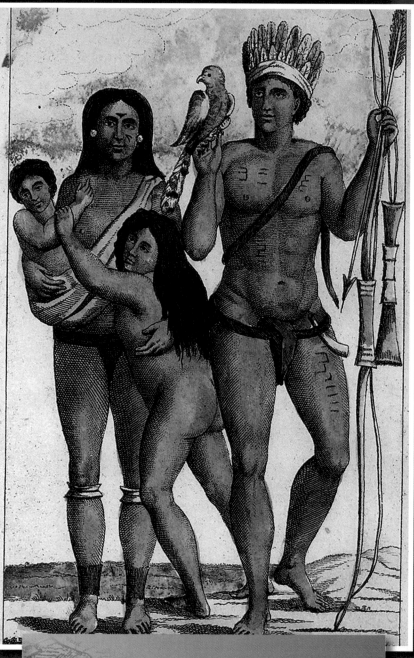

*Famiglia Indiana Caraiba (Caribbean Indian Family)*, painted by John Gabriel Stedman in 1818. Carib Indians inhabited Hispaniola before the Spanish settlers arrived.

If your visit to Parque Colón inspired you to learn more about this country's history, your next stop might be Plaza de la Cultura (Culture Square). That's where you'll find a slew of museums, including the Museum of the Dominican Man, which brings the history of the nation to life. Exhibits there include pre-Columbian artifacts, such as jewelry and sculptures, and other items that showcase Dominican culture.

While Christopher Columbus is credited with discovering the island he would name Hispaniola, he certainly wasn't the first person there. People were living on the island as many as 5,000 years before Columbus arrived! The people, generally referred to as Amerindians, are believed to have arrived on the island from one of two areas. Some are believed to have come from regions in what we call Central America, probably the Yucatán or Belize. Other groups are believed to have traveled farther, probably from areas in what is now known as South America.

If you look at a map, you will see that these tribes or civilizations traveled extremely far in search of a permanent home. No one knows why they moved so far, but they may have been trying to expand their kingdoms, or they were moving away from more aggressive tribes.

The Arawak Indians were from the Amazon area in South America. Scientists believe they traveled north through the area of Venezuela and the Orinoco Valley. Tribes of Arawak Indians merged and married with the tribes from Yucatán and Belize, and the result is the people known as the Taíno Indians.

MIGRATION TO HISPANIOLA

FLORIDA

GULF OF MEXICO

ATLANTIC OCEAN

YUCATÁN

BELIZE

HISPANIOLA

CARIBBEAN SEA

PACIFIC OCEAN

SOUTH AMERICA

The Amerindians who populated Hispaniola before Columbus arrived may have migrated from the Yucatán or Belize, or from the Amazon area of South America.

The word *Taíno* means "good" or "noble" in their language, and it was in that spirit that they greeted Columbus and his men. The Taínos were so peaceful that some of Columbus's men remarked in their diaries that they never saw the Indians even argue with one another or get into fights.

The Taíno culture was a mishmash of the different cultures that came before them. Parts of their society were based on hunting and gathering, while other parts were based on agriculture and farming. They also became accomplished fishermen.

The Taínos called the island *Haiti, Bohio,* or *Quisqueya,* which means "Mother of the Earth." Before Columbus arrived, they had withstood fierce battles with the Carib Indians, who wanted to conquer them; but they were able to hold on to their home.

When Columbus arrived, the Taíno population was divided into five chiefdoms, known as *cazicazgos.* Experts believe they were on the verge of forming a highly organized central government. They wonder whether the society would have flourished or failed had they not been conquered by the Spanish and their advanced weaponry.

Columbus stopped in the Bahamas and Cuba before he set foot on Hispaniola, and he was immediately impressed by the island's beauty. He loved the sheer cliffs, vast mountain ranges, gorgeous beaches, and picturesque river valleys. Columbus wrote about it in his journals.

Unfortunately for the Taínos, their gentle nature made them easy targets for the Spanish invaders. The Spanish took advantage of the Indians, especially after the Taínos revealed that gold and valuable minerals could be found on the island. Remember that the mission of these explorers—including Columbus—was to find gold and other valuables that they could bring back to their own countries.

Around Christmastime 1492, Columbus left a small settlement of about forty men and headed back to Spain. He was eager to tell the queen what he had discovered. But when he returned to Hispaniola several months later, he found that the settlement had been burned to the ground. The settlers had fought among themselves and then with the Taínos—after the settlers had taken advantage of the Indian women.

Throughout Santo Domingo, many of the historic sites still exist— even one of the homes in which Columbus lived. His beautiful mansion rests on the banks of the Ozama River. This twenty-two-room palace became the center of power in the early colonial days, and visiting rulers normally stayed there. Now known as the Alcázar de Colón, it is open as a museum, with many colonial-era treasures on display. The building is also unique in that it draws from many different architectural styles, including Gothic, Arab, and Italian Renaissance.

When Columbus returned to Hispaniola, he started another settlement on the north coast of the island and named it La Isabela, after the queen of Spain. From that area, the Spaniards were able to start mining the country's valuables, including gold.

The Spaniards introduced horses, dogs, armor, and strong weapons to the island, but the deadliest weapon they brought was not one they could wield in battle. They brought germs and diseases to which the Taíno Indians were not accustomed. Because they had never been exposed to these diseases before, the Indians had no immunity to them. They began to perish in great numbers, and the Spaniards conquered them easily.

By the middle of the seventeenth century, the large forces of Spaniards had taken all the gold from the island and began searching for treasure in Mexico. They left behind smaller forces and groups of settlers, and mainly ignored the northwest part of Hispaniola.

During this time period, the English, French, Spanish, and Portuguese were competing against one another for the most colonies and the most wealth. The French set their sights on the nearby island of Tortuga, which is where the pirates of the Caribbean were based—not the ones from the Disney movies, but the real pirates of the Caribbean!

FYI FACT:

The influence of the West African slaves can be found throughout all aspects of culture in the Dominican Republic.

The French also wanted the northwestern part of Hispaniola, which would later be called Haiti. They brought over African slaves to do manual labor there. Over the next 100 years, the French colony became one of the richest in the world.

In the late 1700s, the enslaved Africans revolted and defeated the French. Because Spain had neglected their portion of the island, the liberated Africans took over that side as well. They controlled the entire island for about twenty-two years.

The Spanish ruling class resented being governed by former slaves. They attacked the newly freed people and eventually took back their part of the island. For the next 100 years, brutal Spanish dictators, who revoked personal freedoms, ruled the eastern part of the island. In 1863, the locals forced the Spaniards out and formed the Dominican Republic.

There were valuables other than gold on the island that interested other countries. Sugarcane plantations cropped up throughout the Dominican Republic, and they were gaining interest from American investors. Soon, a lot of money—especially American money—was flowing into the area. To protect its interests, the United States sent marines to the island during World War I under the pretense of protecting it from the Germans.

The Americans stayed for eight years and retrained the local army, including its leader, Rafael Leonidas Trujillo. Once the Americans left in 1924, Trujillo took steps to galvanize his power. By 1930 he was dictator of the Dominican Republic. He ruled for more than 30 years—even though he was accused of terrible crimes, including ordering the slaughter of up to 20,000 Haitians who had been living in the Dominican Republic for years.

The United States looked the other way because Trujillo made favorable deals with the U.S. government and U.S. businesses. But his own people were unhappy with him, and Trujillo was assassinated in 1961.

Today there are free elections in the Dominican Republic, and the people live in relative freedom. Although there are still areas that suffer from poverty, the cities are modern, with tall buildings and paved streets. In the Dominican Republic, as in much of the developing world, you can find the very rich and the very poor. There is normally no "middle class."

Tourists take a cable car to the top of Mount Isabel de Torres. At the top are botanical gardens and a replica of the statue *Christ the Redeemer*, which overlooks the Dominican's northern coast and the city of Puerto Plata.

# Chapter 3

## The Land

Want to experience just about every type of geographical landscape except for the frozen tundra? The Dominican Republic is the place to find them! The country has a wide variety of geographic zones, from rain forests to near deserts. In all there are 27 different climate zones in the Dominican.

There are even several islands that belong to the Dominican Republic. They include the larger islands of Saona and Beata, in addition to two smaller islands, Catalina and Alto Velo.

The northern part of the island rises up out of the Atlantic Ocean, while the southern coast is on the Caribbean Sea. The Mona Passage separates Hispaniola from neighboring Puerto Rico.

Another waterway that draws a lot of visitors—especially between March and January—is beautiful Samaná Bay. The difference between Samaná Bay and other beaches in the country is that you'll want to bring your binoculars when you go. In what is bound to be an experience of a lifetime, you will get to witness the largest congregation of humpback whales in the Caribbean as they migrate through the area. Watching these gigantic yet elegant animals jump out of the water and splash their tails on the surface is remarkable.

After beautiful beaches, coastlines, and whales, the country is probably marked best by the highlands, punctuated by a series of mountain ranges. About 80 percent of the Dominican Republic is mountainous. The mountains are covered by vast and lush forests that keep the soil fertile. This, in turn, allows for productive farming. When making your way through the fertile mountain lands, notice how green everything is!

The largest of the many mountain ranges is known as Cordillera Septentrional. This long range goes from the northern coastal town of Monte Cristi to the Samaná Peninsula in the east. It runs in a straight line parallel to the Atlantic coast, and boasts the four highest mountain peaks in the West Indies. The tallest of these peaks is Pico Duarte, which is 3,087 meters (10,128 feet) high.

If you're interested in a more out-of-the-way spot to explore, try Barahona, which is about a three-hour drive west of Santo Domingo. This area is known for its breathtaking beauty and incredible landscape. There is coastline in addition to mountains, but the real draw is the three national parks located there. One of them, Parque Nacional Jaragua, contains more than 60 different species of birds—including the country's largest flock of flamingos.

Some of the mountain ranges continue on into Haiti, where they are known by different names. They also look very different in Haiti, where the country has been devastated by deforestation. This means that people have chopped down the trees without planting new ones. Deforestation makes the soil infertile and also leads to many mudslides and rockslides whenever there are heavy rains.

While visiting mountain settlements or communities in the Dominican Republic, keep a keen ear out for the rural folk getting together to eat, drink, and sing songs after a hard day's work. This type of mountain folk music is bachata. This slow, melancholy music is usually very simple, with lyrics that talk about daily life in the country, about the struggles of the poor, and of course about love. It is much different than the music you might hear in the bigger cities.

With most mountain ranges, the valleys are low stretches of land between mountain feet. Some of the lowland valleys in the Dominican Republic are very dry and desert-like. In many places in the country, however, the mountains are so close together that the valleys are actually known as highland valleys.

These highland valleys contain a vast amount of fertile land that is perfect for growing food. In fact, some people refer to the highland

During relief efforts after the 2010 earthquake in Haiti, many aid organizations flew into Santo Domingo and drove across the country to get into Haiti.

Like all the other islands located in the Caribbean, the Dominican Republic is a tropical nation. This means it typically experiences warm to hot temperatures year-round, with some heavy-rain seasons and lots of afternoon thunderstorms. Still, temperatures can sometimes dip down to freezing during the winter up in the highest mountain ranges.

The mountains and size of the country actually give it two distinct rainy seasons. On the northern coast, residents can brace for heavy rains between November and January. The remainder of the country can expect the rains to come between May and November. Sometimes the country is hit by tropical storms or hurricanes.

Children take turns jumping off rocks and into one of the three rivers that run through the inland city of Jarabacoa.

# The People

Whether you are dancing your feet off at a local merengue festival or wearing a horned mask during Carnival, the different influences that make up the Dominican people become apparent. On the surface, the people seem to share their cultural identity with other Latin American people. But a closer look will identify the different blend of cultures that have melded together to form the Dominican people.

With more than 10 million people living in the Dominican Republic, the issue of race and background can get a little sticky. The oldest influence is from the Taíno Indians, who later mixed with the Spaniards. The Spaniards enslaved people taken from West Africa. They also imposed a sort of caste system. In a caste system, people are divided into different segments of society and labeled accordingly—from the highest group, the Peninsulares (Spanish colonists who were born in Spain) through merchants and laborers down to slaves. Once in a caste system, a person cannot normally move to a higher or more privileged group.

The caste system sparked racial uneasiness in the Dominican Republic. The racism is surprising, since studies show that more than 70 percent of the population is considered to be multiracial. Less than 20 percent of the population is considered to be white, and about 10 percent is black.

Even after the Spaniards left, the issue of race popped up again under dictator Trujillo, who used racism as a way to spur his party forward. He especially aimed his hatred at the Haitian people, many of whom had moved to the Dominican half of Hispaniola to find a better life. During the Trujillo years, people with dark skin were not treated well. Today, there remain racial problems not only between the Dominicans and the Haitians, but between light-skinned and dark-skinned Dominicans as well.

A 2007 article in *The New York Post* told the story of a black Dominican who waited in line to get into a nightclub. He waited and waited before finally understanding why others were getting in and not he—the color of his skin!

One thing most Dominicans can agree on is religion. Like other areas that were colonized by Spain—a very Catholic country—the Dominican Republic is nearly entirely populated by Christians. Over 90 percent of the people are Catholic, but other religions are also represented, including Judaism.

During World War II, which took place from 1939 to 1945, a wave of European Jews escaped the persecution brought on by Adolf Hitler and the Nazis. Some of them settled in the Dominican Republic and formed their own town, Sosua, on the northern coast.

The Spaniards made Catholicism the basis for all education and required Bible study in public schools. To this day, greetings between friends and relatives are not the typical hello or good-bye, but phrases like *Dios te bendiga* (May God bless you).

Many of the country's festivals and holidays are Christian-based as well. There are patron saints who represent certain areas and who are celebrated at certain times of the year. Two patron saint days are celebrated by nearly everyone on the island: Nuestra Señora de Altagracia (Our Lady of High Grace) is revered as the patroness of the Dominican people, and Nuestra Señora de las Mercedes (Our Lady of Mercy) represents the country of the Dominican Republic.

Every town and city has numerous churches, and big cathedrals are the focus and center of many of them. In plazas that surround the churches, people gather and socialize before and after services.

The religious-based education helped create a learned society. More than 85 percent of the population is considered literate, meaning they can read.

The Cathedral—or, in full, The Holy Metropolitan Cathedral Basilica of Our Lady Holy Mary of the Incarnation—in Santo Domingo is considered to be the first cathedral built in the New World. Parts of the building are made of coral.

School is normally mandatory and free for children between the ages of five and fourteen, though it can be difficult for children who live in mountain villages or very rural areas to get to school. After primary school, there is a two-year intermediate school and then a four-year equivalent of high school. Many of the poorer children cannot attend these schools because their families need them to go to work or because it costs too much money to travel back and forth to school.

Who lives with you in your home? Is it just your parents and brothers and sisters? Some of you may have a grandparent living with you. In the Dominican Republic, a typical family consists of three generations living together. It is customary to allow the oldest male to run the family and make all the public decisions. The oldest married woman runs the household and makes decisions there. Family is very

Traveling to school can be expensive. In many rural small towns, the people travel by horse, donkey, or mule.

The houses in the Dominican Republic are very simple and have dirt floors. When the dirt gets loose, it needs to be swept out the door.

important in the Dominican Republic, and most people rely on family members for nearly every part of their lives: friendship, social functions, and even financial matters.

Like most former Spanish colonies, the main language in the country is Spanish. In the areas of the Dominican Republic where there is a lot of tourism, some of the people speak English and maybe other languages as well. However, you would be hard-pressed to find anyone who speaks English outside the major cities.

A statue of Dominican baseball legend Sammy Sosa stands in front of Plaza 30-30, a shopping center that Sosa built in the town of San Pedro de Macorís.

# Culture and Lifestyle

Riding down most any street in the Dominican Republic, you are bound to see kids playing baseball. Dominicans are friendly, gregarious people who love good food, company, fast music, the arts, literature, and maybe above all else—baseball.

America's national pastime is probably more popular in the Dominican Republic than it is anywhere else in the world, including the United States and Japan, where professional leagues color the sports pages and fill stadiums. Maybe the sport does not generate as much revenue there, as it does in the United States, but it sure dominates Dominican society.

The Dominican Republic is second only to the United States in producing Major League ballplayers. Is there a Major League Baseball training center near where you live? If you lived in the Dominican Republic, the answer would be yes. Every American Major League Baseball team has opened training centers in the Dominican as they look for the next José Reyes or Pedro Martínez! They teach the kids to play and let them work on their skills.

The sport was introduced to the country in the 1860s mainly by Cubans fleeing their own country. U.S. Marines had introduced the game to Cuba, and from there it spread throughout the Caribbean.

The sport really took off in the southern part of the country, when sugarcane plantation owners encouraged their workers to play the game during the sugar season's slow time. They even sponsored teams that would play against other farms in the area. That's similar to how the sport spread in the United States as well—with factory owners instead of plantation owners sponsoring teams and encouraging their employees to play.

It is not uncommon to spot a baseball park or kids playing ball anywhere in the Dominican Republic. The passion for the sport is so high that kids even play the game when they cannot afford to buy equipment. Many notable Major League players, like Sammy Sosa, often speak about learning the game by using a cardboard baseball mitt, socks or rocks for the ball, and a tree limb as the bat.

Of course Dominican culture exists off the baseball diamond as well. Do you hear that music blasting out of the nearby car radio or from the shop next door? That pulsating, fast-paced music is called merengue. It is known by its steady beat, which combines African rhythms with European melodies. The music is predominantly performed by three-piece bands consisting of an accordion and drummers to keep the beat. It typically has between 120 and 160 beats per minute.

If you are lucky enough to go to the annual Merengue Festival at El Malecón near the port of Santo Domingo, make sure to try some of the authentic local cooking as well. All that dancing is bound to get you hungry.

When it comes to food, Dominican cuisine is among the tastiest in the Caribbean. Many of the dishes are similar to those in Cuba and Puerto Rico, former Spanish colonies as well, with Taíno and African influences. Rice, beans, pork, and spices are staples of daily life in this country, along with the heavy use of plantains—a type of banana. Plantains—boiled, fried, or roasted—may be served with just about every meal.

**FYI FACT:**

Since the early 1990s, a type of Dominican rap music has emerged, especially among the younger people, known as Rap Del Patio (street rap, or yard rap). Like American rap music, Rap Del Patio focuses its lyrics on urban life, money, crime, and women. Reggaeton music is also popular among the Dominican people.

A traditional chicken stew cooks in a large cauldron at a house in the Dominican countryside.

Other popular side dishes are root-type vegetables such as cassava. The root vegetables were introduced by enslaved Africans during colonial times. A typical breakfast in the Dominican Republic is eggs and mangu—a boiled and mashed root vegetable—along with plantains.

The most typical lunch dish in the country is *la bandera* (the flag). This is broiled chicken served with steaming hot white rice and red beans with sauce.

Save room for dessert. Dominican treats feature just about anything sweet, from rice puddings and custards to sweet creamed beans and even a piece of sugarcane known as *caña*. Meals are typically topped off with freshly squeezed fruit juices and strong Dominican coffee, grown on the island's mountain ranges.

Don't forget to support the arts while you are there as well. For only a few dollars you can buy a street painting from a local artist, some beautiful terra-cotta pottery, or painted hand-carved gourds.

A piece of amber with a perfectly preserved spider. The Dominican Republic is one of the main sources of amber in the world.

*Chapter*

# 6

# Economy and Commerce

Have you ever seen the movie *Jurassic Park*, or maybe you read the book? It is about a scientist who was able to extract the DNA of dinosaurs from mosquitoes trapped in resin millions of years ago. The mosquitoes bit the dinosaurs and then were preserved for all those years in the fossilized resin called amber. Using the dinosaur DNA trapped in the mosquitos and DNA from frogs, the scientist tried to re-create dinosaurs for a theme park. Part of the *Jurassic Park* movie was filmed in the Dominican Republic, and right after the release of the film, amber sales increased by 500 percent.

While it may not be possible to re-create dinosaurs, amber is very real. It is considered a gem, like diamond or pearl, even though it is not a mineral. Nowhere in the world is there as much amber as in the Dominican Republic.

Several active mines extract amber from the earth, and it is sold throughout the country. Amber glows under blacklight, so make sure you buy it from a dealer who offers you a chance to see it under one of these special lights.

The country has one of the best and fastest-growing economies in Latin America. It has the largest economy in all of Central America and the Caribbean. Besides the mining of amber and precious metals, the main forces that drive the economy are the service industry—which includes tourism—and agriculture.

Tourism accounts for more than a billion dollars annually for the Dominican economy. White sand beaches, pristine water, and modern resorts draw tourists from all over the world—some of whom arrive by cruise ship. And even though the island nation is forever dealing with power shortages and blackouts, the hotel industry is well supplied. Nearly all the resorts have generators to make sure that guests are never left in the dark.

Because tourism is so important, there are numerous festivals and celebrations throughout the year. Whenever you decide to visit, there will probably be a festival going on.

One such festival that takes place in the Dominican, and other Caribbean nations as well, is Carnival. This celebration marks the beginning of Lent, a period of reflection in the Catholic tradition. Carnival takes place in the capital city of Santo Domingo, and like other Carnival festivals, people dress up in colorful costumes and wear masks of funny imaginary creatures and scary monsters. These masks are known as *diablo cojuelos* (demons), and there is a contest for the best one. There are also plenty of wildly colorful floats in a parade that is the highlight of the festival.

The tourism industry—including hotels, restaurants, bars, shops, and other services—is the biggest employer in the Dominican Republic, providing about 750,000 jobs. Major resorts continue to be built, and these will drive those numbers even higher. There are at least 70,000 hotel rooms on the island. While most people visit the country to relax on the beautiful beaches, there is also a growing eco-tourism industry for people who want to stay in lodges and hotels in the mountains and other natural areas.

Even though tourism is the biggest moneymaker, the industry that is most important to the island's well-being is agriculture. The most important crop in the country is sugarcane.

Sugarcane originated in Asia and the Far East. It was introduced in Europe long before Christopher Columbus decided to plant some in the Caribbean in 1493. The first sugarcane fields in the Dominican Republic began producing in 1501. The first varieties of sugarcane produced sweet stalks that people chewed on fresh from the fields. For hundreds of years sugar has been grown mainly in the southern plains of the country.

Today the Dominican Republic ranks second only to Cuba in producing sugarcane in the Caribbean. In the late 1980s and early 1990s, the island produced more than seven tons of sugarcane a year. This number dropped steadily in the early 2000s as farmers tried to make more money growing other crops.

The next most popular crop is coffee. The rich mountain soil is perfect for growing coffee plants and producing beans. A 2001 study showed that the country generated $11 million per year growing and exporting coffee to other countries.

Tobacco and cocoa beans are the next most abundant crops. In fact, the Dominican Republic is one of the top ten cocoa producers in the world. Other crops include rice, coconuts, and bananas. Farmers also raise goats, sheep, cattle, pigs, and chickens.

Besides amber, the most popular resources mined in the Dominican are nickel and ferronickel. In the 1970s, the most productive gold mine in the entire Western Hemisphere was found in Pueblo Viejo (Old Town) in the Dominican Republic. Before that, U.S. companies mined the metals necessary to create aluminum. There is also copper on the island, as well as one of the world's biggest natural salt deposits. Since 1993, there have been calls from some in the government and by environmentalists to slow down the mining and work on planting trees instead. They are afraid of deforestation, which is to blame for many natural disasters in the neighboring country of Haiti.

Because of their proximity and intertwined histories, the biggest trading partner of the Dominican Republic is the United States. Other countries that trade with the Dominicans include Canada, some western European nations, and Japan.

FYI FACT:

More than 90 percent of Dominican exports come to the United States.

Even though the Dominican Republic is far more advanced than many other Latin American countries, it is still a developing country with a lot of poverty. Almost 16 percent of the population remains unemployed.

Just a few miles from the beautiful resorts in Santo Domingo are sprawling slums that show the immense poverty in this developing country.

# Politics and Government

The people in the Dominican Republic are very passionate about their politics and are not afraid to show their support. In 2004 I took a trip to the Dominican Republic to report about a flash flood that killed thousands of people. While we were driving, I noticed that a lot of things were painted purple. There were rocks, signs, utility poles, and many other objects painted purple. I later found out that purple was the color of one of the parties running for government offices in an election. I also learned that someone running for president had tried to bribe everyone in the country with a free bottle of beer if he was elected!

When looking at the fabulous resorts and hotels, it is sometimes easy to forget that this country is a developing country with many problems. Politicians have their hands full, whether it's dealing with undocumented workers or the power outages that plague most of the country. It is not uncommon to see wires going from house to house as people steal electricity. A law was passed making that practice illegal, but it has not been enforced. The Dominican Republic also faces the problem of undocumented workers—people who sneak into the country illegally to work at hard-labor jobs. People from Haiti sneak across the border to work in the sugarcane fields.

No one has had more influence over the Dominican government than former dictator Rafael Trujillo. His answer to undocumented workers was simply to order the massacre of Haitians living on the Dominican side of the border.

Despite his iron-fisted way of ruling, Trujillo was beloved by many. The United States had backed him for many years but shunned him after he tried to have the president of Venezuela assassinated.

After Trujillo himself was assassinated, the United States tried to help the Dominicans establish a democratic government, including elections for their leaders. But when a left-leaning president was elected, the United States intervened and helped overthrow him. Years of indecision and unrest followed, and when it appeared that pro-Castro or communist revolutionaries might take over the country, U.S. President Lyndon B. Johnson sent American troops to the nation.

In Cuba, Fidel Castro and the Communist party confiscated property, factories, and investments owned by Americans. Johnson was afraid that would happen in the Dominican Republic, so he sent soldiers there to prevent it. The troops stayed in the Dominican Republic for a year, and in 1966 the people elected Joaquín Balaguer as president. This would be the true start of free elections in the country—even though Balaguer did not allow the people many freedoms. He felt it was more important to keep the communists from taking power. While he had a poor record when it came to human rights, Balaguer is credited with helping to bring the country into the twentieth century. Making it a priority to improve the country's infrastructure, he built schools, roads, reservoirs, highways, theaters, and museums. Balaguer was reelected in 1970 and 1974. Incredibly, he was elected again in 1986 and 1990. But in the late 1980s the country suffered through an economic depression and a very tough time. People became angry when basic things like water, electricity, and transportation systems began to fail. There were protests everywhere that sometimes turned violent. In June 1989 there was a nationwide strike to protest the impoverished conditions.

Today the government of the Dominican Republic is modeled after the U.S. system. It is divided into three equally powerful parts—the executive branch, the legislative branch, and the judicial branch. The legislative branch is made up of two houses: the Senate and the Chamber of Deputies.

While the U.S. political scene has two major parties—Democratic and Republican—the Dominicans have three major parties from which

Dominican President Leonel Fernández Reyna and his wife, Margarita Cedeño de Fernández, visited with U.S. President Barack Obama and his wife, Michelle, in September 2009.

to elect their leaders: the Social Christian Reformist Party, the Social Democratic Dominican Revolutionary Party, and the Dominican Liberation Party. Elections are held every two years, alternating between legislative and presidential. While many elections in Latin America and other third-world countries are mired in accusations of fraud or intimidation, that is not the case in the Dominican Republic. International observers have monitored elections since 1996, and they say the elections have been fair and free.

The Dominican president may have a little more power than people are accustomed to in the United States. In the Dominican Republic, the president appoints each of the governors for the 31 different provinces or states. The people are able to vote for mayors and town councils that handle local matters.

President Leonel Fernandez Reyna was reelected in 2008 to a four-year term. His party, the Dominican Liberation Party, has been in control since 2004. Long known as a nation allied with the United States, the Dominican government sent military to troops to assist the U.S. in Operation Iraqi Freedom in 2004. The country's military is fairly large, and its navy, which protects the waters surrounding the nation, boasts 12 ships. Of all the countries in the Caribbean, only Cuba has a larger navy.

Baseball superstar and Dominican native Albert Pujols celebrates with his son moments after helping the St. Louis Cardinals win the 2006 World Series.

# Famous People

The Dominican Republic has been the home of many famous people, from politicians and poets to power hitters in baseball.

### Juan Pablo Duarte

Juan Pablo Duarte was born on January 26, 1813, and is considered by many to be the founder of the Dominican Republic. Duarte was known as a liberal thinker who believed in the principles of democracy.

In 1801, when the Spanish left the Dominican Republic and the Haitians took control of the entire island, Duarte's parents moved to nearby Puerto Rico. His childhood was spent learning about the Haitian occupation and the need for the Dominican people to have independence.

In 1838, Duarte and a few others formed a secret patriotic society called La Trinitaria, which was used to help move the independence movement forward and to harass the Haitian occupiers. This movement—along with the work of other freedom fighters who led the call for independence—finally led to the declaration of independence in 1844. By this time, however, Duarte had been banished from the country for his actions and was living in Venezuela. He tried to get involved in Dominican politics, but his political career never advanced. While he spoke of an independent democratic nation, his fellow countrymen wanted to go back to reliance on Spain. He died July 15, 1876.

## Rafael Trujillo

Despite his reputation as a cold-blooded ruler, no look at famous Dominicans would be complete without a closer look at dictator Rafael Trujillo. He was born October 24, 1891, to a middle-class family in San Cristobál. He went to school and obtained a basic education. Unsuccessful in finding a steady job, Trujillo began training as an officer in the National Guard, an organization that had been created by the United States.

Trujillo was a natural soldier and soon rose in rank and power. In 1924 he was named second in command of the troops. Only a year later he became the commander in chief.

There was much unrest in the country in 1930, and protesters were calling for the president to resign. General Trujillo stayed out of the conflict and remained neutral. Once the president stepped down, Trujillo announced that he was running for president. After having many of his opponents jailed or beaten, he won the election. He had many monuments built in his honor and also changed the names of many cities and streets to his own.

He served as president from 1930 to 1938, and again from 1942 to 1954, then chose his brother to succeed him. But he was always in charge of the country even during the few years that he was not officially president.

Trujillo confiscated many businesses in the country or forced owners to make him a business partner. He amassed a fortune even though his people lived in poverty. He was assassinated in 1961.

## Fabio Fiallo

Poet, writer, and journalist Fabio Fiallo was born on February 3, 1866. His career as a poet was cut short because of his political activism. Over the years, Fiallo founded four newspapers and fought constantly for a free press. In many countries, newspapers are not allowed to publish what they want. As a journalist he wrote many articles advocating liberty for the Dominican Republic from U.S. soldiers, who occupied the nation at various points in history.

Even his poems and short stories were full of calls for a free government, more rights for the people, and freedom of speech. He was an outcast in his country and even imprisoned many times for his beliefs, and many people called him a traitor. That did not stop him. Finally he fled the country and lived out his years in Cuba, where he died in 1942. His remains were brought to the Dominican Republic in 1977, and he was honored as a hero.

## Julia Alvarez

Dominican writers and poets have traditionally kept to their Spanish and European influences, especially the well-known literary Henriquez-Ureña family. Since the end of the twentieth century, however, they have been leaving the European influences behind and creating a style of writing that is purely Dominican. One writer who has done this successfully and enjoyed some popularity is Julia Alvarez. A writer and poet, Alvarez was born in New York City on March 27, 1950, then moved to the country of her parents, the Dominican Republic. Her father was a doctor who helped run a local hospital in the 1950s. When it was discovered that he was involved in a plot to overthrow Trujillo, her father had to escape from the country with his family.

They settled in New York City. Alvarez has had a successful career writing about her experiences in the Dominican Republic and in the United States. Her most famous work is a novel called *How the Garcia Girls Lost Their Accents*.

Alvarez earned her college degree and also became a college professor. Her second novel, *In the Time of Butterflies,* is about three sisters who were assassinated during Trujillo's last days as dictator. The book was a critical success and won several awards. Alvarez has also written several volumes of poetry about the Dominican experience.

## The Alou Brothers

While the Dominican Republic boasts a large number of Major League Baseball players competing in the United States—including such well-known superstars as Vladimir Guerrero and Albert Pujols—the most well-known band of baseball brothers ever to play the game are the Alou brothers.

Baseball slugger Vladimir Guerrero would be a candidate for the baseball Hall of Fame when he retired.

The oldest of the brothers, Felipe, dreamed of escaping poverty by one day becoming a doctor. However, while participating as a track runner in the Pan American Games, he decided to try his hand at baseball and was a natural.

Felipe, Matty, and Jesus Alou played professional baseball from the 1950s to the 1970s. They are the only trio of brothers to ever start a game in the same outfield. On September 10,

The baseball-playing Alou brothers made history by playing all three outfield positions for the San Francisco Giants in 1963.

1963, the three of them played the outfield for the San Francisco Giants and even batted in the same inning, setting a record that will likely never be matched.

Felipe and Matty each made Major League All-Star teams. Felipe later became the first Dominican to be named manager of a Major League Baseball team. Adding to the legacy of the Alou brothers baseball story, Felipe's son, Moises Alou, enjoyed a long career as a power-hitting baseball player as well.

Long stretches of sparsely populated beach are perfect for horseback riding.

# Chapter 9

## Festivals and Attractions

Because of the country's beautiful and varied landscape, there has been a growing interest in ecotourism—visiting a natural habitat or some ecological wonder. Tour a rain forest, or go horseback riding, kayaking, scuba diving, or snorkeling.

Sports nuts can watch baseball games throughout the year, enjoy sport fishing off the coast, and in June check out the annual World Cup competition of windsurfing. The event takes place in Cabrete and lasts about three weeks. The final week of competition consists of an international race as well as concerts and parties.

There are many deep-sea fishing opportunities in the Dominican Republic, including the White Marlin Tournament every June in Punta Cana. Hundreds of boats go out, hoping to land the wondrous sportfish known for its long tail-walks and acrobatic leaps out of the water. To ensure that there is always great fishing off the coast, most marlin are tagged and released. Photos are taken by the captain so that you can have a replica of the fish made and mounted on your wall at home. Now that's a souvenir!

If you're fascinated by fossils and haven't had your fill of amber yet, enjoy the Amber World Museum. Emilio and Manolo Perez started mining amber for sale in

**A white marlin**

the 1940s. Dominican amber—unlike Baltic or Mexican amber—almost always has something inside the pieces, ranging from termites and prehistoric ants to grasshoppers and flowers. At first they threw away all the pieces that had things preserved in them, because they didn't think people would want the amber unless it was pure. Then they realized they were throwing away the more interesting pieces. One amber piece in the museum contains a 17-inch- (42.5-cm-) long lizard!

No visit to the Dominican Republic would be complete without really diving into the music of this passionate nation. There are merengue festivals throughout the country, but the largest festival is held in October in the city of Puerta Plata.

During Carnival time, party revelers dress up in colorful costumes and hats. They participate in parades, contests, games, and dancing.

A man wears the mask of *diablos cojuelos* as part of a Carnival celebration at Fort Ozama.

This celebration is half music and half gigantic harvest festival. Hundreds of vendors travel to the festival to show and sell their clothing, crafts, crops, or other foods. The streets are closed to traffic, and a large stage is built at the end of the road. This is where the country's most famous merengue singers perform concerts for the duration of the festival.

Another festival where visitors can learn about Dominican culture is the Holy Week Festival that takes place every year in the town of Sosua. This week before Easter Sunday is filled with volleyball competitions, dancing, concerts, and lots of traditional food.

A fifteenth-century Spanish knight in armor is on display at the Museo Alcázar de Colón, one of several great museums in Santo Domingo.

Fishing, sunbathing, hiking to mountain villages, whale watching, and even shopping for precious amber make for a great vacation, but the Dominican Republic has much more to offer. In fact, most visitors will tell you that one of the most amazing parts of their trip is seeing the history as it is preserved throughout the country, especially in the colonial city of Santo Domingo.

Some of the architectural highlights include The Cathedral, which is the oldest standing church in all the Americas. It was constructed between 1514 and 1542, and it stands near the giant statue of Christopher Columbus in Parque Colón. The church is complete with stained glass created by a Dominican artist.

For a look at a typical colonial street, take a walk down Las Damas Street. Many of the buildings are constructed of cement-like mixtures that contain crushed seashells. At the very end of the picturesque block are Ozama Fortress and Tower of Heritage. The fort was built in 1503, the oldest military outpost in all of the Caribbean and Latin America. It has hints of medieval style combined with traditional Spanish architecture.

Another magnificent site is the San Francisco Monastery Ruins. Built by Franciscan priests from the Roman Catholic Church, it is believed to be the first monastery built in the New World.

To get a great view of the city and of many historical sites from one point, take a walk on El Callejón de los Curas (The Alley of the Priests). This little walkway goes behind the oldest cathedral in the

Americas to the cloisters. Along the way, visitors can spot numerous colonial buildings and interesting sites.

One particular spot to visit and really feel the history is the Casa del Cordón, or the Cord House. The house was built twenty years after Columbus arrived and was the first Spanish-style building to be constructed in the country. It is also the oldest structure in the New World with two floors. The beautifully ornate front door is framed by what appears to be a huge rope belt, but it is actually made of stone. The "rope belt" honors the Franciscan order of Catholic priests who were very influential during that time. The impressive structure was once the home of Diego Columbus, Christopher Columbus's son. Diego's two sons were born there.

Fort Ozama was built by the Spaniards to deter attacks by the English and by pirates.

Many of the city's historical sites such as the Casa del Cordón, impose dress codes. Visitors are asked not to wear shorts, short skirts, T-shirts, or flip-flops.

Over the years, many influential people lived in the Cord House, holding state functions and important parties there. When English pirates temporarily invaded Santo Domingo, negotiations between pirates and the Spaniards took place in the house. The building now serves as a cultural center.

Another fun historic house to visit is the House of Medallions, built around 1540. It got its name because of five medallions with human faces inside the building. There is one medallion on each of the two pillars near the entrance, and the remaining three are in the wall above the doorway. The center face is that of a child who is believed to be King Carlos V.

Nearby is one of the oldest structures on the island of Hispaniola. The Casa de Francisco Tostado was built in the fifteenth century. Tostado, who had the house built, was one of the earliest Spanish settlers to arrive. He was a well-known writer whose son—Francisco Tostado de la Peña—became a very famous writer. The home, with lavish construction, is one of a kind in the country. The top floor has a view of the ocean.

Many influential people lived in the house, including Francisco Rodríguez Franco and the Archbishop of the Catholic Church. The government took it over in 1970 and made it a historical monument. Now a museum, it holds many important historic documents.

After discovering the history and fun in Santo Domingo, head back to your hotel for a swim in the pool or just to lie out on the beach. The Dominican people are happy for your visit.

**Dominican Recipe**

### Dulce de Leche en Tabla
### (Milk Fudge Bars)

This tasty treat, which is a staple for kids in the Dominican Republic:

8 cups fresh milk or full cream
8 cups brown sugar
1 teaspoon grated lime peels

1. Line a small cake pan with waxed paper.
2. Mix the milk and brown sugar in a deep iron or aluminum pot.
3. **Ask an adult** to help you boil the milk and sugar over medium heat. Keep stirring. Cook until the milk looks like it is getting firm. Be careful not to let the pot boil over.
4. Add the lime peels. Stir the mixture constantly until it looks like yogurt or pudding. Turn off the heat.
5. Pour the mixture into the cake pan. Let the mixture sit for at least two hours. Once it has hardened, cut the fudge in bite-sized squares and serve.

## Make a Dominican Decorative Plate

Material needed:
- 1-inch sponge brush
- 6-inch clay saucer
- light green and dark green acrylic paint
- household sponge
- black permanent marker
- scrap paper
- computer with Internet connection (optional)
- black construction paper
- scissors
- gloss decoupage medium

1. Using the sponge brush, paint the saucer light green. Allow it to dry completely.
2. Using a small piece of a household sponge, dab dark green paint over the light green color. Dab lightly so that the light green shows through. Let it dry.
3. Use your imagination or artistic talent to draw designs around the outside edge of the saucer with the black permanent marker.
4. Using scrap paper, draw a symbol that you would like to see on the plate, or go online and look up Taíno symbols. Then trace the symbol onto black construction paper.
5. Use scissors to cut the symbol out.
6. Glue the symbol onto the center of the saucer using the decoupage. Apply several coats over the symbol and the surface of the saucer. Allow each coat to dry before adding the next one.

| | |
|---|---|
| 1492 | Christopher Columbus visits the island, which he names "Little Spain," or Hispaniola. |
| 1496 | The Spaniards set up the first Spanish colony in Western hemisphere at Santo Domingo, which later is recognized as the capital of all Spanish colonies in South America. |
| 1697 | The Treaty of Ryswick gives the western part of Hispaniola, now known as Haiti, to France and the eastern part, now the Dominican Republic to Spain. |
| 1821 | A revolt against Spanish rulers is followed by a brief period of independence. |
| 1822 | Haitian President Jean-Pierre Boyer marches his troops into Santo Domingo and annexes it. |
| 1844 | Boyer is overthrown, political leaders in Santo Domingo declare their independence, and the Dominican Republic is formed. |
| 1861–63 | The Spaniards return and once again claim the area as a colony. |
| 1863–64 | Spain leaves for a second time after a revolt and once again the people claim independence. |
| 1916–24 | U.S. military forces occupy the Dominican Republic after a period of unrest. |
| 1930 | General Rafael Trujillo becomes dictator of the country after the overthrow of President Horacio Vazquez. |
| 1937 | Trujillo orders the massacre of 20,000 Haitians living in areas of the Dominican Republic near the border. |
| 1961 | Trujillo is assassinated. |
| 1965 | 30,000 U.S. troops invade the country following more unrest and a fear that the country will adopt a communist form of government. |
| 1966 | Joaquin Balaguer is elected president. |
| 1996 | Leonel Fernandez Reyna of the leftist Dominican Liberation Party (PLD) elected president. |
| 1998 | Hurricane George ravages the island. Baseball slugger Sammy Sosa hits 66 home runs. |
| 2002 | Former president Joaquín Balaguer dies in July at the age of 95. |
| 2004 | More than 2,000 near the border with Haiti are killed during floods. |
| 2008 | President Leonel Fernández Reyna is reelected in May. |
| 2010 | President Reyna organizes an aid commission to help Haiti after it is struck by a devastating earthquake. The Dominican Republic provides health care, water, electricity, military assistance, and other aid. |

# FURTHER READING

## Books

Gritzner, Charles F., and Douglas A. Phillips. *The Dominican Republic.*
Philadelphia, PA: Chelsea House, 2010.

Haberle, Susan. *Dominican Republic.* Mankato, MN: Capstone Press, 2004.

Rogers, Lura, and Barbara Radcliff Rogers. *The Dominican Republic.* Mankato,
MN: Children's Press, 2008.

Temple, Bob. *Dominican Republic.* Broomall, PA: Mason Crest, 2008.

## Works Consulted

Aunt Clara's Kitchen Dominican Cooking
http://www.dominicancooking.com/

Brown, Isabel Zakrzewski. *Culture and Customs of the Dominican Republic.*
Westport, CT: Greenwood Press, 1999.

Chandler, Gary Prado, and Liza Prado Chandler. *Dominican Republic.*
Melbourne, Australia: Lonely Planet Publishers, 2002.

"Dominican Republic Amber"
http://dr1.com/articles/amber.shtml

Pons, Frank Moya. *The Dominican Republic: A National History.* Princeton, NJ:
Markus Wiener Publishers, 1998.

Porter, Darwin. *Frommer's Portable Dominican Republic.* Hoboken, NJ: Wiley
Publishing, 2009.

Tavarez, Julio. "The DR's Dark Secret: Racism Against Black Dominicans Has
Become Epidemic on the Island." *New York Post*, August 8, 2007
http://www.nypost.com/p/lifestyle/tempo/item_WrhrYnQsu34MpaieKpJpIM

## On the Internet

Dominican Republic
http://dominicanrepublic.com/index.php

Dominican Republic Ministry of Tourism
http://www.godominicanrepublic.com/

Lonely Planet: Dominican Republic
http://www.lonelyplanet.com/dominican-republic

U.S. Department of State: Dominican Republic
http://www.state.gov/r/pa/ei/bgn/35639.htm

PHOTO CREDITS: Cover, pp. 32, 54—Adam Jones; pp. 2-3—Cláudio Lisian Santos; p. 3—Clyde Bentley, p. 20—Ruben Laguna; p. 30—Ken Mayer; p. 31—Michelle Brea; pp. 43, 45, 46, 47—Library of Congress; p. 49—AP Photo; p. 53—AP Photo/Ramon Espinosa; p. 56—John Connell. All other photos—Creative Commons. Every effort has been made to locate all copyright holders of material used in this book. If any errors or omissions have occurred, corrections will be made in future editions of the book.

**amber** (AM-bur)—The hard yellow fossilized resin of trees.

**cassava** (kuh-SAH-vah)—A root vegetable introduced to the Caribbean by African slaves.

**caste** (KAST)—The dividing of people into categories depending on who their parents are or how much money they have.

**colonial** (kuh-LOH-nee-ul)—Describing the people who have taken land that once belonged to someone else and making it their own; also, describing the land taken that way.

**confiscate** (KON-fih-skayt)—To take something away from someone for legal reasons.

**Creole** (KREE-ohl)—The language spoken by Haitians, consisting of French, Spanish, and African languages.

**deforestation** (dee-far-es-TAY-shun)—Cutting down trees and not replacing them, and therefore leaving the land bare.

**democracy** (deh-MAH-kruh-see)—A governmental system in which the people have the power through electing representatives.

**dictator** (DIK-tay-tor)—A person who rules with total authority.

**environmentalist** (en-vy-urn-MEN-tul-ist)—A person who is concerned about ecology and controlling pollution.

**fertile** (FUR-til)—Land that has the nutrients for growing a lot of crops.

**Peninsulare** (pay-nin-soo-LAY-ray)—Dominican colonists who were born in Spain.

**plantation** (plan-TAY-shun)—A large area on which a certain crop is grown.

**poverty** (PAH-ver-tee)—Very poor, not having what society says is enough to live.

**tournament** (TOR-nuh-munt)—A contest for a championship.

**tyrant** (TY-runt)—Someone who rules a country with absolute power and who may use brutality to enforce his or her power.

# INDEX

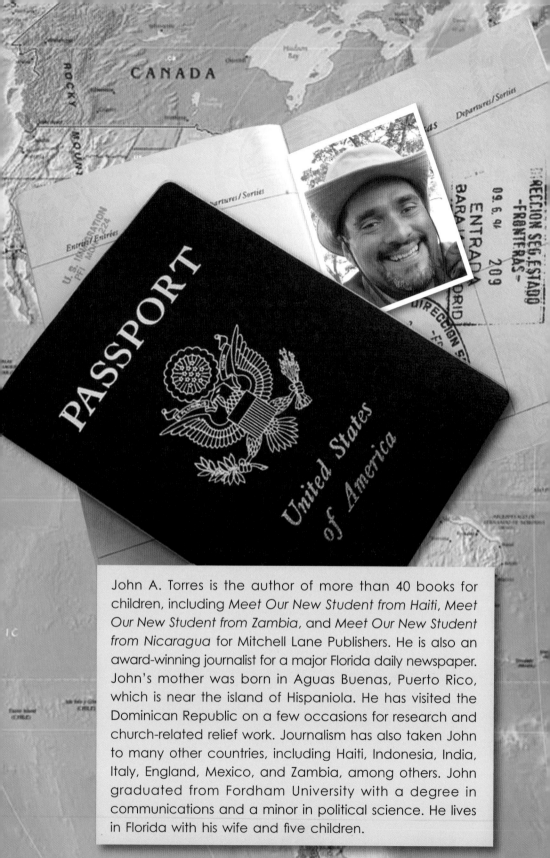

John A. Torres is the author of more than 40 books for children, including *Meet Our New Student from Haiti*, *Meet Our New Student from Zambia*, and *Meet Our New Student from Nicaragua* for Mitchell Lane Publishers. He is also an award-winning journalist for a major Florida daily newspaper. John's mother was born in Aguas Buenas, Puerto Rico, which is near the island of Hispaniola. He has visited the Dominican Republic on a few occasions for research and church-related relief work. Journalism has also taken John to many other countries, including Haiti, Indonesia, India, Italy, England, Mexico, and Zambia, among others. John graduated from Fordham University with a degree in communications and a minor in political science. He lives in Florida with his wife and five children.